Financial Management Made Manageable

Financial Management Made Manageable

Bryan Mills

Bryan Mills
2017

First Printing 2017

ISBN ISBN 978-0-244-01932-7

Bryan Mills

Helston Cornwall UK

www.drbryanmills.com

Contents

Preface

After spending 20 years lecturing financial management on degrees and professional courses (ACCA, CIMA, CMI) I came to realise that a concise text focusing on the most likely maths problems students encounter would be welcome. In this text I have tried to move swiftly to calculation and to application. I have sought to explain these calculations from first principles, and as such some readers may wish to skip sections or even chapters, and I have aimed to explain methods in as clear a way as possible. This text is aimed at both undergraduate and post-graduate students and is designed to be read alongside, not instead of, longer and more theoretical texts.

I have covered the basics of financial management from calculating the cost of equity and debt to investment appraisal and futures contracts. The reader will note that I have left uncovered issues relating to governance and financial conduct and codes. This is intentional and in the spirit of a text that seeks to cover quickly and clearly the aspects of financial management that in my experience students find difficult.

Dr Bryan Mills BA(Hons), DipFM, PGCE, Phd, MIfL, SFHEA

Mills (2017) Financial Management made Manageable

Understanding Equity

Introduction

In order to understand financial management it is necessary to get to grips with the way companies are funded. The money in a company that pays for capital expenditure (machines, plant, property, etc) and working capital only has two sources. It is either borrowed (covered in later chapters) or belongs to the company owners. Regardless of whether it is new money introduced, existing holdings or retained profits the money that is not introduced as debt is referred to as equity.

To be able to understand the returns a company is required to make we must have an understanding of the owners' desired returns – after all it is their company. Their returns will be the company's costs. By calculating these required returns we can ascertain the target for any new investment and judge the success of existing investments.

It is worth noting that there are differences in company ownership and these have a bearing on the cost of equity. At the simplest level the sole trader or business partnership can arbitrarily decide on a target figure based on their own requirements and expectations. Likewise a Ltd company may select a target figure by discussing at board level what is required. It is only the Plc that has data that can be used to determine actual costs of equity as it is only them that have equity that is traded regularly and therefore priced in a market. It is of course possible, desirable even, for sole traders, partnerships and Ltd companies to use estimates based on Plc values to provide a range of estimates, and these are covered in the chapter on WACC, but this is not necessarily common practice.

This chapter will begin by exploring the Efficient Market Hypothesis in order to better understand the way markets price equities. It will go on to calculate the cost of equity using two models – the Dividend Valuation Model and the Capital Asset Pricing Model.

The Efficient Market Hypothesis (EMH)

At the heart of financial management and the determination of cost of capital is a belief in efficient markets for equity and debt. To be able to price capital reliably there must be a mechanism to establish a value in a market place – without exposure to the rigour of a fluid market the cost of capital would higher. This is evident in the value of unlisted firms (firms not on the stock exchange). These firms are typically lower in value and hence higher in yield for investors (and higher in risk) and therefore cost for the company.

To be confident that a market is efficient we need to be confident that prices accurately reflect value. That is to say what we pay for a share reflects the business risk associate with that type of industry and the financial risk associated with that company's gearing along with protection from the time value of money (as we have locked our money up in an investment we need to be 'compensated' for loss of value due to inflation and loss of the ability to use that money – an opportunity cost).

With the idea that we need a market to establish prices and that to be efficient this market needs to be reliable and accurate it follows that we can set up a series of hypotheses to test various assumptions about that market. These falsifiable statements allow us to test our assumptions against empirical evidence. The three basic assumptions are that the market is random; the market reflects all publically available information; the market reflects all information (public and private). These are referred to in turn as the Weak-form; Semi-strong-form and Strong-form (this theory was put forward by Eugene Fama in 1970[1]).

If the weak form were found to be valid then share price would follow a random walk. That is to say that neither news stories nor past price movements have any effect on share price. Even a casual glance at stock market indices and share prices would show that the market seem to follow trends – either a slow upward trend over a period of weeks or months or perhaps a roller-coaster ride over a few hours – what is clear is that the prices are not behaving randomly. Add to this the clear response to news releases – whether these are macro events such as political change or micro events related to that specific market or company – it is clear that (new) information can impact share price.

This takes us on to the second of the three hypotheses. The semi-strong hypothesis asserts that share prices respond to publically available data, and that it does so rapidly. As such investors cannot make excessive returns from new information simply because that information is quickly reflected in the share price. Fundamental analysis (investing based on company data) or technical analysis (investing based on statistical interpretation of share price movements) cannot lead to gains for the investor. The semi-strong hypothesis is generally regarded as the most realistic interpretation of price movements.

The final hypothesis, the strong-form hypothesis, implies that prices also include private information. This is to say that information held within firms and not made public is also reflected in share price. Apart from the fact that there is legislation to prevent this sort of insider dealing we have also seen over a number of years numerous examples of companies that have managed to

---

[1] Fama,, E., (1970). Efficient Capital Markets: A Review of Theory and Empirical Work. *Journal of Finance.*, Vol. 25, No. 2: pp. 383–417.

hide information from the market. This would include Parmalt, Enron not to mention the sub-prime market of the mid-2000s. Whilst we have stated that the semi-strong-form is the most 'likely' that is not to say it is proven. Critique and contrary evidence of EMH comes from behavioural economists, from evidence of bubbles and from the late 2000s' financial crisis. Behavioural economists point out the very human nature of trading and our susceptibility to various biases which influence the way we process data. Both bubbles and the financial crises demonstrate that the market can get prices very wrong.

Practical implications of EMH:

- Timing of financial policy (for example rights issue/initial public offering) – in theory the best time to sell new shares would be when the market is high. If EMH holds true the manager cannot know what represents high (tomorrow's figures may be higher or lower). In addition there is also no point waiting for today's low to pick up – we have no way of knowing it will.
- New project evaluation – net present value calculations (covered later in text) often uses the returns expected on other similar investments as a guide to a realistic return - this only works if EMH holds true and companies that have similar business and financial risks produce similar returns.
- Creative accounting – any attempt at massaging figures or 'spinning' company performance will fail as investors will eventually see through such tricks and will adjust their interpretation of the data accordingly.

- Mergers and take-overs - the price of a share will reflect a zero NPV. In other words the return will reflect risk and a fair return and provide the investor with a secure investment but no more. Thus the only way to gain through merger or acquisition is through cost efficiency.

- Validity of current market prices - there is no need to discount new issues and no such thing as an undervalued share –there are no 'buy now's'.

The Dividend Valuation Model

The first of two methods to calculate the cost of equity (k_e) that we will consider is the dividend valuation model (DVM). As the name suggest the model uses dividends to calculate either share price or the cost of equity depending on what is being sought. DVM makes use of four values: the share price, the dividend, the cost of equity and the growth in dividends. Depending on which three of these are provided the fourth can be calculate.

Starting at first principles it should be reasonable clear that if a share costing £1 pays a dividend of 10p then the return is 10%.

$$\frac{£0.10}{£1.00} = 10\%$$

As the company is paying the dividend the return is in fact a cost to it. In other words the cost of capital is 10%. This works unless the investment is for a period longer than one year. In the case of investments that go on for more than one year (and companies are expected to have a lifespan beyond one year) both the pattern of dividends and the final sale price of the share need to be considered.

If we were to simply suggest that each year we receive 10p for our initial investment of £1 we will have mistakenly ignored the time value of money. In five years' time what now cost £1 will cost more, we will have lost the opportunity to invest the money elsewhere and we will have been exposed to risk of never making a return. In addition we have not included a calculation that allows for dividends to grow in coming years. The first of these problems, time value of money, is solved by discounting the future earnings. This is explained more fully in the chapter on investment appraisal but an introduction is provided below:

Compound interest:
Assume an investment of £100 that pays 10% for five years

Year 1 £100 @ 10% = £110
Year 2 £100 @ 10% = £121
Year 3 £121 @ 10% = £133.10
Year 4 £133.10 @ 10% = £146.41
Year 5 £146.41 @ 10% = £161.05

If we use decimals instead of % we can more conveniently write this as:

£100.00 x1.10 = £110.00
£110.00 x 1.10 =£121.00
£121.00 x 1.10 =£133.10
£133.10 x 1.10 =£146.41
£146.41 x 1.10 =£161.05

We use 1.1 to represent 100% (1) of the invested money and 10% (0.1) of the return (interest). Another way of writing the above would be £100 x 1.1 x 1.1 x 1.1 x 1.1 x 1.1 = £161.05

And of course the easiest way to write that is £161.05 = £100x 1.1⁵. This allows us to say that the formula for compound interest is:

FV = PV (1+r)ⁿ

Where:
FV = future value
PV = principal value (investment)
r = rate of interest
n = number of years.

Whilst this gives us future value it can also be reversed to give present value:

FV = PV (1+r)ⁿ

Becomes:

$$PV = \frac{FV}{(1+r)^n}$$

If we were to look at a series of dividend payments it would look something like this – each time we divided it is by a higher number (the powers are increasing by 1 each time) further reducing the value of the dividend:

$$P_0 \leq \frac{D_1}{(1+r)^1} + \frac{D_2}{(1+r)^2} + ... + \frac{D_n + P_n}{(1+r)^n}$$

Where P_0 is present share price, D_n is dividend and r is return (or cost k_e). The final term, P_n, would be the final sale price of the share. This expression translates to: the present share price should be equal to or less than next year's discounted dividend plus the year after's discounted dividend, plus the year after, etc. until the share is sold.

It is very unlikely you would be asked to calculate a share price in this way. What this model shows is what is theoretically happening. In practice and in examinations this approach is shortened. To do that two assumptions are made. First those dividends grow at a constant rate and second that the sale price is so far off in the future that its value is effectively zero in today's terms. This then provides us with the following formula in which growth in dividends is represented by g and r (return) is replaced with k_e (cost):

$$P_0 = \frac{D_0(1+g)}{K_e - g}$$

$D_0(1+g)$ represents this year's dividend growing at a rate of $1 + g$ or in other words next year's expected dividend. This is sometimes rewritten as:

$$P_0 = \frac{D_1}{K_e - g}$$

Where D_1 represents next year's dividend.

So the current price of a share (P_0) can be estimated by examining the present dividend (D_0), the required return on equity (K_e) and the rate of growth (g). If we rearrange this formula we can determine what the cost of equity is assuming we have a current share price.

Cost of Equity using DVM:

$$K_e = \frac{D_0(1+g)}{P_0} + g$$

Note that when calculating you must use a share price that is ex-div. That is to say the dividend has just been paid. The reason for this is shares increase in value as they approach the dividend date. If you are given a cum div value for the share simply subtract the dividend from it.

There are certain assumptions with this model. First dividends grow at a constant rate and are paid in perpetuity. Second that the market is efficient and third that share price represents discounted future cash flows.

Example:

A company's shares are trading at £3.00 the dividend of 20p is about to be paid and these have been growing at 2%. What is the cost of equity?

Note that the share is cum div – that is the dividend is about to be paid. Thus we have to reduce the share price by the dividend making £3.00-£0.20 = £2.80. Now we can use the formula:

$$K_e = \frac{20(1+0.02)}{280} + 0.02 = 0.093 \text{ or } 9.3\%$$

Note: use either pounds or pence for both monetary values.

In an exam you may not be given the rate of growth. If that is the case one can be estimated, providing you are given a range of dividends, using the formula:

$$1 + g = \sqrt[n]{\left(\frac{D_0}{D_{-n}} \right)}$$

In other words 1 plus the rate of growth equals the nth root of (this year's dividend divided by the old dividend) where n is the number of years difference between old and new dividends.

The Capital Asset Pricing Model (CAPM)

The dividend valuation model relies on past information relating to dividends and current information relating to share price to estimate the cost of equity for a company. To a large extent this is a very insular calculation that makes little reference to the wider market. If we were to consider the behaviour of investments in the wider market we would see that there were often two elements to their movements. The first can be termed systemic. This is when the whole economy or market (the system) moves and the company moves with it. Companies may over-react to movements or may under-react. Industries that under-react tend to sell staples and utilities that people buy regardless of changes in the economy. The second element is change related to the individual company's behaviour and performance. This can be referred to as unique or un-systemic risk.

If an investor were to hold a portfolio – that is a collection of investments in different companies or assets – then they would be able to diversify away some of the unique risk – particularly if the investments chosen did not correlate with each other. In fact it has been shown that providing the portfolio has approximately 15 to 20 different and uncorrelated investments most of the unique risk is diversified away and the portfolio represents the system or market risk – in other words it behaves like an index tracker[2].

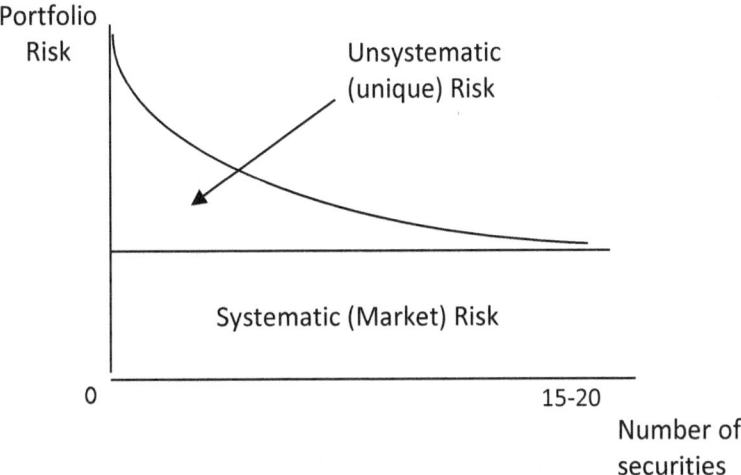

Based on the assumption that there is both systemic and unsystemic risk it is possible to measure the relationship between each investment's return and the return of the overall market. There will be some sort of covariance between these two values that allows a judgement to be made as to whether the investment is over- or under-reacting (or mirroring – i.e. matching).

In an exam it is common to be given this value. The value is referred to by the Greek letter beta or β. If you are required to calculate it, and this would only be required in an advance course of financial management study, then the method is as follows:

---

[2] Evans, J. L. & Archer, S., H. (1968) Diversification and the Reduction of Dispersion: An Empirical Analysis, *The Journal of Finance.* Vol. 23, No. 5, pp. 761-767

$\beta_{\text{security } j} = \dfrac{\text{systematic risk of security (j)}}{\text{market risk (m)}}$

Given that the systematic risk is the relationship between the security and the market - the correlation - the numerator in the formula must contain this correlation and risk. Risk is given as the standard deviation of return – shown by the σ (sigma) symbol - and correlation is shown using the ρ (rho) symbol. This combination of correlation and risk is known as covariance:

$$\beta_{\text{security } j} = \frac{\rho_{j,m}\sigma_j}{\sigma_m}$$

In most cases this value will be given to you and outside of exam situations it can be found on most financial websites that detail company information. Once we have a value for beta we can use this to determine the expected return from the company. In the chart below you will see that the lowest ever expected return would be the return from a risk free investment (R_f) – such as a deposit savings account or a government bond. As these are low risk they have low returns.

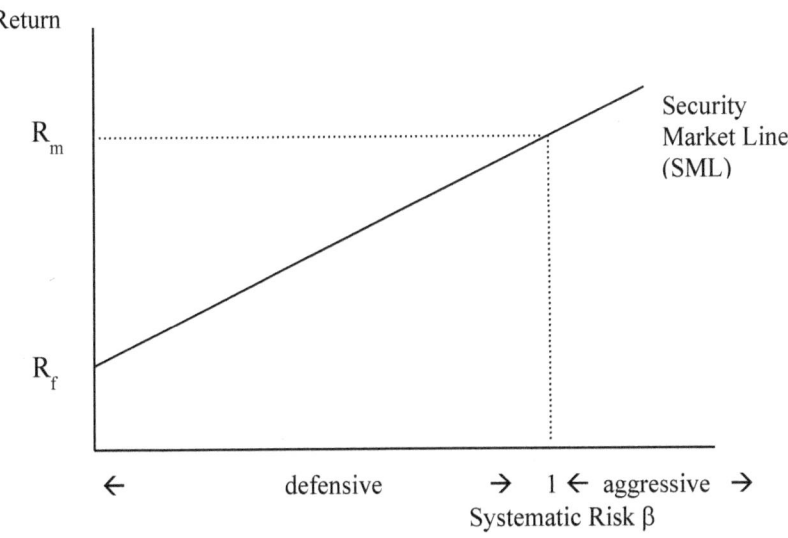

All investments will expected to be higher than R_f. If the investment mirrors exactly the market then its return will be the same as the market – R_m. In this case the beta value would be 1. Some investments may over perform – and have higher betas (these are called aggressive) and some may underperform and have lower betas (defensive). Note that this is not necessarily a bad thing. These defensive betas do not rise as high but they also do not fall as low.

This information allows us to build the CAPM. Starting with R_f as our lowest value we know that CAPM must be higher than this – so CAPM begins $R_j = R_f + \ldots$ where R_j is the return on investment j (and this return becomes the cost we are looking for k_e).

We also know that the amount higher will be some proportion of the difference between risk free and market returns. Perhaps it will be defensive and half the difference or aggressive and something like one and half times the difference. This will depend on the Beta value calculated or given. Thus the formula becomes risk free return plus some proportion of the difference between the market return and the risk free return.

Cost of Equity using CAPM:

$R_j = R_f + \beta_j(R_m - R_f)$

R_j = expected return (k_e)
R_f = risk free return (given as the return on deposit accounts or government bonds)
R_m = market return (given as the return on a market index – FTSE, DOW, S&P etc)
β_j = beta value (probably given in exam or calculated as above)

As with DVM there are certain assumptions used with CAPM. Again it is assumed that there is an efficient capital market. In addition it is assumed that there is unrestricted borrowing at the risk free rate of return and that there is a uniformity of investor expectations (see earlier comments on behavioural economics). In addition it is assumed that the forecast is based on a single time period.

This leads to certain limitations including the assumption that unsystematic risk is avoided by assuming a diversified portfolio. In addition it only looks at return in the most simple of ways (rate of return not split into growth, dividends, etc.) and is based on one-period. It can also be difficult to estimate the terms used in the model (R_f R_m β) and generally is not thought to work well for investments that have low betas, seasonality and low PE ratios - partly because it overstates the rate of return needed for high betas and understates the rate needed for low betas.

However CAPM does have some advantages over DVM namely it provides a market based relationship between risk and return and demonstrates the importance of systematic risk. In addition it can be used to risk adjusted discount rates for project appraisal (see later in chapter on WACC).

Example:
A company has a beta value of 1.5. The average return from the FTSE is 10% and government bonds are yielding 2% what is the cost of equity?

$R_j = R_f + \beta_j(R_m - R_f)$

$k_e = 2 + 1.5(10 - 2)$
$k_e = 2 + 1.5 \times 8$
$k_e = 2 + 12$
$k_e = 14\%$

Mills (2017) Financial Management made Manageable

Understanding Debt

Introduction

Now that we have established a value for equity we need to determine the required return of our debt holders. In some cases this is as simple as the required return on a loan. In this case whatever money is left over after the interest has been paid forms part of our retained profits. Whilst this is straightforward enough in degree examination you are often asked to consider the case of bonds and/or debentures. These forms of debt add a complication as they are not a simple contracts between you and the lender. Instead a bond/debenture is a tradable security that has a value that will go up and down relative to a market. This in itself has little practical implication for the company on a daily basis as it pays interest (called a coupon) based on the bond/debentures par value (the face value of the bond – normally £100) regardless of what the bond/debenture is presently trading for. However it does alter the cost of the bond.

This chapter will explore the use and cost of short and long term debt and will demonstrate how to calculate the cost (or yield) of a bond/debenture. The calculations used in this section are helpful as they are reused in the chapter on Investment Appraisal to calculate internal rate of return (IRR).

Short-term debt

Companies, like people, often rely on short term debt. In the case of a company these can be approximated to debts that appear on a balance sheet for less than one year (though they may be rolled over they are incurred, paid and incurred again). The two most common short-term debts (sources of finance) are overdrafts and credit (accounts payable). However it may also include unpaid taxes and short term loans. Short term debt is not normally examined in investment appraisal projects and is normally considered a way of funding working capital. Some organisations do fund working capital (net current assets) using long term finance as it is common for a company to roll over working capital such that it becomes a permanent current asset (a company will grow current asset value as it expands).

For the purposes of investment appraisals, rather than accounting, short term debt is generally considered flexible (in both directions) but suitable only for small amounts (relative to company size) and temporary investments.

Long-term bank debt

Where a company requires money for periods longer than one year it may use bank loans. These loans are either secured (have ownership of an asset attached to them which can be used in the event of foreclosure) or unsecured. In a domestic situation it is likely that the mortgage on your home is secured (in fact that is the definition of mortgage) and your car loan is unsecured. Secured loans will attract lower interest payments as there is less risk for the investor. It is not uncommon to have covenants on loans, particularly business loans that restrict any behaviour that may alter the liquidity of the company. The loan will be for a fixed term, usually with repayments of capital plus interest on a monthly basis and that interest will either be fixed or variable.

Debentures and Bonds

Larger companies, and organisations and governments, often raise money by selling bonds or debentures. A debenture is unsecured and a bond is secured on assets. In an examination you are likely to be asked to calculate either the yield of a bond/debenture or the cost of debt. In both cases the same calculation is used – all that differs is the way tax is treated. Bonds and debentures are calculated in the same way.

Unlike a bank loan a bond is not repaid monthly and does not consist of an agreement to receive and then repay a certain amount of money normally at regular monthly intervals. Instead bonds have what is called a par (face) value of £100 and a coupon stated as a % based on that £100. In addition they have a maturity date. Some bonds are irredeemable – that is to say only the coupon is paid no repayment of capital occurs whilst others are redeemable, usually at par value and this repayment occurs at the maturity date. Bonds can also be bought and sold after issue and are not necessarily sold at £100.

Based on this we could expect to see, for example, a redeemable bond that has five years until maturity with a coupon of 3% trading at £96. Basically this means that if you pay £96 for the bond you will receive £3 (£100 x 3%) for five years and in the final year you will also receive £100. It is immediately apparent that the yield (return) or cost is not 3%. Not only does £3 not represent 3% of £96 it also does not take account of the time value of money of the final value of £100.

If we present the values in a table it becomes clear:

Year 0	Year 1	Year 2	Year 3	Year 4	Year 5
(£96)	£3	£3	£3	£3	£103

A total of £115 is received but this is spread over five years. As such the later values, including the repayment at par of the capital, needs to be discounted. If we knew the exact cost of capital that converted those five years' worth of values into £96 we would know the yield. This value can be calculated using interpolation (something that will be used again in determining the IRR in the chapter on Investment Appraisal).

To estimate the yield (see note at end of section on tax and cost of debt) we need to discount the values using a cost of capital. Though there is no rule to doing this a fair starting point is to try the coupon as a discount rate.

	Year 0	Year 1	Year 2	Year 3	Year 4	Year 5
CF	(£96)	£3	£3	£3	£3	£103
DF	1	0.971	0.943	0.915	0.888	0.863
CF x DF	(£96)	£2.91	£2.83	£2.75	£2.67	£88.85
					NPV	£4.00

The discount factors (DF) are obtained from a table of discount factors or from the formula below the table. These decimals have the effect of lowering the value of the coupon to allow for time:

Cost of capital

Year	1%	2%	3%	4%	5%	6%	7%	8%	9%
1	0.990	0.980	0.971	0.962	0.952	0.943	0.935	0.926	0.917
2	0.980	0.961	0.943	0.925	0.907	0.890	0.873	0.857	0.842
3	0.971	0.942	0.915	0.889	0.864	0.840	0.816	0.794	0.772
4	0.961	0.924	0.888	0.855	0.823	0.792	0.763	0.735	0.708
5	0.951	0.906	0.863	0.822	0.784	0.747	0.713	0.681	0.650
6	0.942	0.888	0.837	0.790	0.746	0.705	0.666	0.630	0.596
7	0.933	0.871	0.813	0.760	0.711	0.665	0.623	0.583	0.547
8	0.923	0.853	0.789	0.731	0.677	0.627	0.582	0.540	0.502
9	0.914	0.837	0.766	0.703	0.645	0.592	0.544	0.500	0.460
10	0.905	0.820	0.744	0.676	0.614	0.558	0.508	0.463	0.422

$$DF = \frac{1}{(1+r)^n}$$

Where r = discount rate as decimal and n = number of years.

The NPV (net present value) is simply the sum of the bottom row. This calculation has shown that 3% is not a high enough value to balance the cash flows in with the original cost. Put simply if the cost of capital was 0% then the money in would be £115 which is £19 higher than the money out (£96) – this would clearly be wrong as we have a return higher than 0 as a £19 return on £96 does not equal zero. We now recalculate the table using a higher cost of capital (we will try 5%). If the NPV had been negative we would have used a lower cost of capital.

		1	2	3	4	5
CF	Year 0	Year 1	Year 2	Year 3	Year 4	Year 5
DF	-£96	£3	£3	£3	£3	£103
CF x DF	1	0.9524	0.9070	0.8638	0.8227	0.7835
	(£96.00)	£2.86	£2.72	£2.59	£2.47	£80.70
					NPV	(£4.66)

We now have four values. At 3% we have an NPV of £4.00 and at 5% an NPV of (£4.66). The actual yield (cost) is somewhere between these two values. A mathematical technique called interpolation can be used to determine the exact value.

If we were to visualise what we are trying to do it would look like this:

3%	?%	5%
£4	£0	(£4.66)

We are aiming to determine the % that will give us £0 and show that the cashflow in exactly balances the original cashflow out.

The value will be at least 3%, in addition it will be somewhere between 3% and 5%. So it will be 3% plus some fraction of the difference between 3% and 5% (i.e. some fraction of 2%).

This can be written as:

$$Yield = 3\% + \left[2\% \times \frac{£4}{£4 + £4.66} \right] = 3.92\%$$

Notice that the minus sign has been dropped from the £4.66 this is because the range (distance) between £4 and (£4.66) is what is required.

$$Yield = \text{lowest \%} + \left[\text{difference in \%} \times \frac{\text{Positive NPV}}{\text{Range of NPV}} \right]$$

It should be remembered that the above calculation are for yield. Yield is from the perspective of the investor. The same calculation is used to find the cost of debt (k_d) but to do so the coupons need to be adjusted by the rate of tax. If the rate of corporation tax was 30% in our example above the coupon would be adjusted from £3 to £3 less 30% (the easiest way to do this is to multiply by 0.7 which is (1-t)). So in our example the coupon cashflow would be £2.10. This will clearly alter the final value. In fact the cost of debt is always less than the yield. This is because a company is able to claim its interest payments as an expense and this reduces its tax liability.

The Weighted Average Cost of Capital (WACC)

Introduction

Although we now have both a cost of equity and a cost of debt we still do not have a single figure we can use to assess the viability of new and existing investment opportunities. In much the same way that a student's grade is determined by combining results from a collection of assignments so a company's cost of capital is determined by averaging the cost of equity and debt whilst adjusting for relative proportions.

This chapter demonstrates how to calculate the weighted average cost of capital (WACC) before going on to discuss some of the theoretical underpinnings. The chapter ends by adjusting the WACC to allow for changing financial risk (the risk associated with that level of gearing) to the original company on which the calculation was based.

The WACC calculation

The WACC calculation is surprisingly simple, given the calculations used in previous chapters. If we start by assuming a company is all equity financed then the pool of capital for the company consists of only equity and so the WACC is equal to the cost of equity.

In an all equity company:

$WACC = k_e$

This may be the case in some smaller private companies but it is more common for companies to have some debt (the reasons for this are explained later in the chapter). If we had a company that was half equity and half debt – in other words its balance sheet was funded by equal parts debt and equity - then the WACC would simply be the average of the cost of equity and the cost of debt. In other words it would be:

$$WACC = \frac{k_e + k_d}{2}$$

Which is the same as WACC = k_e x ½ + k_d x ½

In this case the equal parts equity (1) and debt (1) are divided by 2 to find the average. Any other proportions are also possible simply by replacing the numerators by the relevant values of equity and debt respectively and the denominator by the sum of equity and debt (total capital).

For example with the following values:
k_e = 10
k_d = 4
E = £120m
D = £30m
We get:

$$WACC = \frac{10 \times 120}{120 + 30} + \frac{4 \times 30}{120 + 30} = 8 + 0.8 = 8.8\%$$

Based on the formula:

$$WACC = \frac{k_e \times E}{E + D} + \frac{k_d \times D}{E + D}$$

It is important to note that k_d in this example is based on having calculated the cost for a bond. If the exam question was using bank loan interest then that needs to be adjusted for tax (1-t) as we did for the coupons above (k_d would be $k_d(1-t)$).

It may be the case that in the exam question you are not told the total equity or debt (or at least not the market values of these which are required to calculate WACC). Providing you are given three pieces of information (book value, par (issue) value and market value of the individual security) it is possible to calculate total market value.

For example:

A company's share price is £1.50 and the bond value £96.
The balance sheet looks like this:
Issued share capital (£0.50) of £10million
Bonds of £2million

To convert this to market values we simply divide the book value by the par value and multiply by the market value. Note that we do not need to be given the par value for bonds as it is always £100 (as discussed in section on cost of debt above).

Equity $= E = (10m \div 0.5) \times 1.50 = 20 \times 1.50 = £30m$
Debt $= D = (2m \div 100) \times 96 = 0.02m \times 96 = £1.92m$

As can be seen the equity value is above book value as the shares now trade at a price above par and the debt is lower as the debt is trading below par.

Theoretical underpinning of the traditional approach

One of the assumptions we make with calculating WACC is that the cost of equity will increase as the level of gearing (the size of D relative to E) increases. This assumption is based on the theory that as gearing increases so does financial risk and as a result equity investors demand higher returns. This means that although we can 'swap' expensive equity for cheaper debt there will come a point when this advantage begins to reverse. This point will be the cheapest WACC and is termed the optimal capital structure.

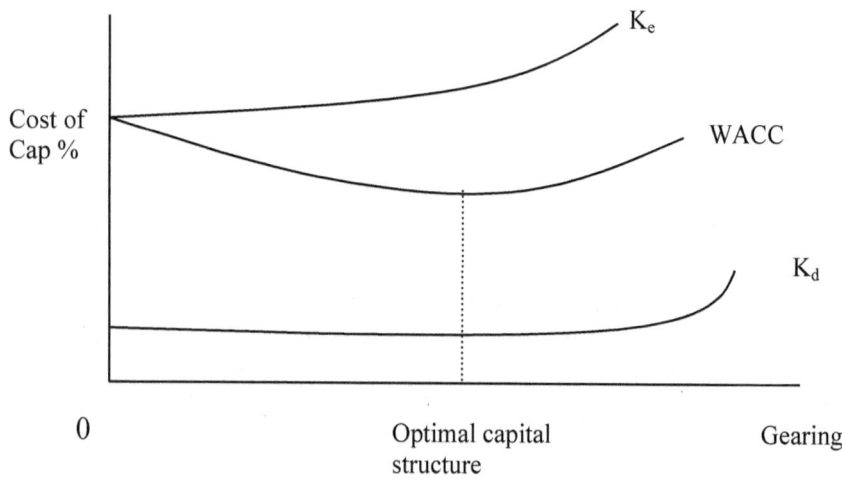

The more debt introduced the lower the WACC, even though the equity investors are having to be compensated for increasing risk. Eventually the cost of this compensation gets too much, in addition lenders can also start to demand more at high levels of gearing.

The optimal capital structure represents a minimised return to investors (debt and equity). This point also maximises the value of the firm's debt and equity and maximises its value (it is after all paying the lowest possible cost in terms of finance and so is maximising retained profits).

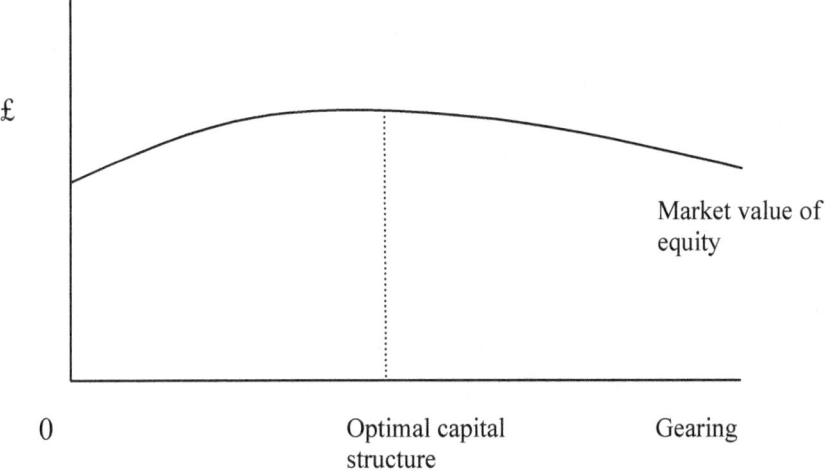

Exam question may ask for ether the structure that minimises WACC or maximises the value of the firm - they are the in effect the same question.

There are some limits to this theory. It only works when gearing is not expected to alter. If gearing alters not only does E and D alter but K_e will also need to be recalculated. This is because financial risk (gearing) is not ignored by investors. In addition if a new project (a new direction adopted by the business that has necessitated changes to gearing) is in an market that the company does not presently operate in then there is a change to business risk (effectively a change to the unique risk discussed in the section on CAPM) and this will have an impact on the k_e in addition to the effect caused by alteration to gearing.

Modigliani and Miller

Modigliani and Miller challenged the traditional view of capital optimisation in a 1958 paper published in the American Economic Review[3] and later updated in 1963. Though this may seem dated and the actual debate around their proposal seems to take us back to the traditional view it is an important and useful avenue to explore. What they managed to achieve was a deepening of our understanding of capital structures and through that they have facilitated better business decisions.

The Concept of Financial Risk

As previously mentioned there are two main risks that we can examine in this context. Business risk is the risk implicit in doing that type of business and financial risk which is the risk introduced by gearing.

There are 3 ways of looking at this:

Pecking Order, The Traditional Approach (as covered above in the section on WACC) and the Modigliani & Miller approach (M&M)

Pecking Order:

We first fund new projects with retained profit/internally generated funds, if that is used up we seek to use debt and finally we may seek additional equity (beyond retained profits). In other words this approach is not based on optimal capital structure but on minimising administrative (transaction) costs (i.e. easiest first).

---

[3]Modigliani, F .& Miller, M. (1958). "The Cost of Capital, Corporation Finance and the Theory of Investment". *American Economic Review*. Vol 48, No 3, pp 261–297.

Modigliani, F.& Miller, M. (1963). "Corporate income taxes and the cost of capital: a correction". *American Economic Review*. Vol 53, No 3, pp 433–443.

Traditional:
As discussed above debt finance can lower WACC until an optimum is reached.

Modigliani & Miller:
This approach argues that gearing has no effect on the cost of capital and so all capital structures are optimal.

The theoretical case for all structures being optimal

Modigliani and Miller proposed that companies which operate the same type of business and which have similar operating risks (i.e. similar business risk) must have the same value, irrespective of capital structure. In this case the only thing that matters is future operating profits.

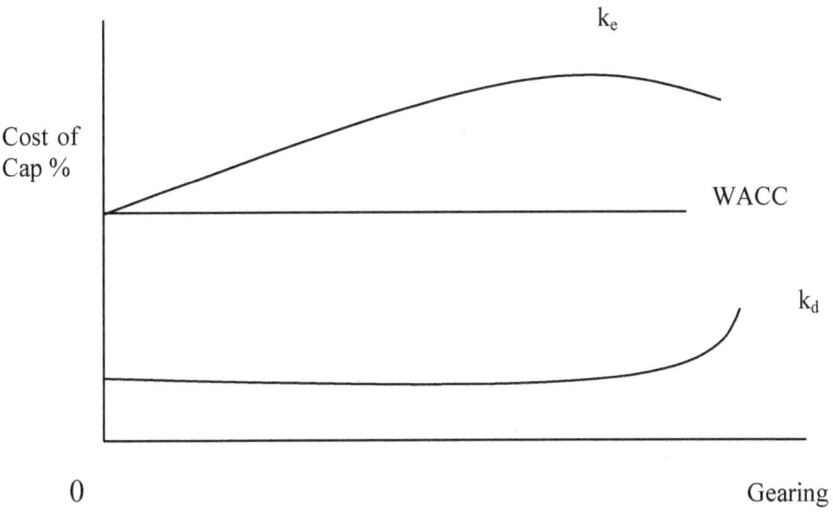

Any benefit the firm gets from using cheaper debt is offset by dearer equity. Thus the firm is indifferent to capital structure as all are optimal.

33

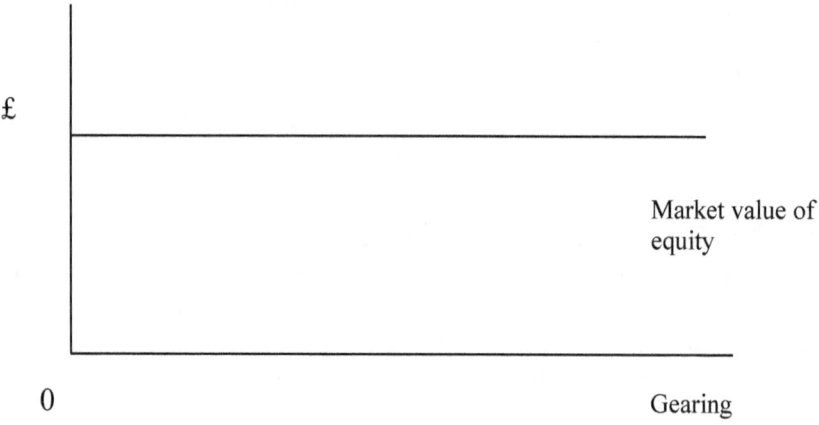

$£$

0 Gearing

The Arbitrage Process

This is explained by referring to the concept of arbitrage. Arbitrage means buying in one market to sell in another and relies on discrepancies in those markets to profit.

For example:

Equity Plc & Gear Plc both have the same business risk and both generate £10,000 pa before interest

Equity Plc is equity financed and has equity market capitalisation of £100,000

As the earnings are paid as dividend then cost of equity is £10,000/£100,000 = 10%

Gear Plc has £40,000 worth of debt at 5%. You would 'traditionally' expect Gear Plc to have lower combined cost of capital and a higher total market capitalisation (debt + equity).

Assume this is £120,000

Therefore equity is £120,000 - £40,000 = £80,000

If you had 10% of Gear Plc and sold it for £8,000 and then borrowed £4,000 @ 5% you would have the same gearing as Gear Plc. Gear Plc is £80,000:£40,000 equity:debt and you are £8,000:£4,000 equity:debt.

Using this £12,000 you could buy 10% of Equity Pklc and have £2,000 left over

Your net dividend with Gear Plc would have been:

	£
Earnings before interest from Gear Plc	10,000
Less interest 5% on £40,000	2,000
Available for Dividends	8,000
As a 10% shareholder	800

Now with Equity Plc it will be:

	£
Dividends from Equity Plc (10% of £10,000)	1,000
Less interest on loan 5% on £4,000	(200)
Net receipts	800

Spare funds = £12,000 - £10,000 = £2,000
Same return, same risk but with money to invest elsewhere!
This would surely attract people to do the same thing and sell shares in Gear Plc meaning their price would fall and buy shares in

Equity Plc meaning their price would rise until there was no advantage in buying and selling.

This is called the net operating income argument and basically means that the combined cost of capital is unaffected by the level of gearing. As such it remains constant at the cost of equity of an ungeared company with the same business risk

Criticism of the 1958 Modigliani and Miller model

However there are some criticisms of the 1958 model. First market inefficiencies prevent arbitrage working well, in the same way that the cost of equity, debt and WACC discussed above are limited by the assumption that the market is efficient this model also has that restriction. However in this case the need to buy and sell to take advantage of arbitrage makes that even more pronounced. In addition it is clear that personal borrowing is not a perfect substitute for corporate borrowing. The interest you are likely to be charged compared to a company with a strong track record and numerous assets is unlikely to be favourable. The model also ignores taxation. Companies have tax relief on interest payment whereas private citizens do not and of course selling shares to take advantage of arbitrage has capital gains tax implications which lower the returns.

Tax and Modigliani and Miller 1963

In 1963 another paper was published that sought to address the tax issue. As debt interest can get tax relief, geared companies pay less tax and this should lead to a greater market value and lower WACC.

For example:

	Equity Plc	Gear Plc
	£	£
Equity	100,000	80,000
Debt		40,000
	100,000	120,000
EBIT	10,000	10,000
Interest		(2,000)
EBT	10,000	8,000
Tax @ 30%	3,000	2,400
Earnings available to equity	7,000	5,600

The cost of equity for Equity Plc can be estimated:
7,000/100,000 = 7%

The cost of equity for Gear Plc can be estimated:
5,600/80,000 = 7%

As you have 10% of Gear Plc and are concerned that there is more risk in geared companies you could sell these shares. The company only really pays £1,400 (£2,000 x 70%) interest, of which your 'share' is equivalent to £140. To keep risk constant when exchanging corporate for personal gearing you would be looking for a debt interest of £140.

This suggests £140/5% = £2,800 borrowings. The tax has reduced this from the previous example from £4,000 to £2,800 and subsequently the spare funds is reduced from £2,000 to £800. It may still be attractive to switch from Gear Plc to Equity Plc but the arbitrage advantage will be shorter lived. To cancel out the £800 Gear Plc's equity would have to fall in value by £8,000 (as £800 is 10% of £8,000). This would give £40,000 (debt) + £72,000 (equity) = £112,000. This is still higher than the ungeared firm due to the benefits of tax relief.

The annual tax advantage brought about by debt can be said to be:
Debt x interest rate x tax rate
Written as: Dit

If this is in perpetuity then it is: $\dfrac{Dit}{i}$

which cancels to Dt

So using the debt and tax rate from above:

£40,000 x 0.3 = £12,000

This market values relationship between two firms that are identical except for gearing can be expressed as:

Vg = Vu + Dt
Where:
Vg = market cap of geared (debt + equity)
Vu = market cap of ungeared
D = debt
t = tax rate

Dt is often called the tax shield

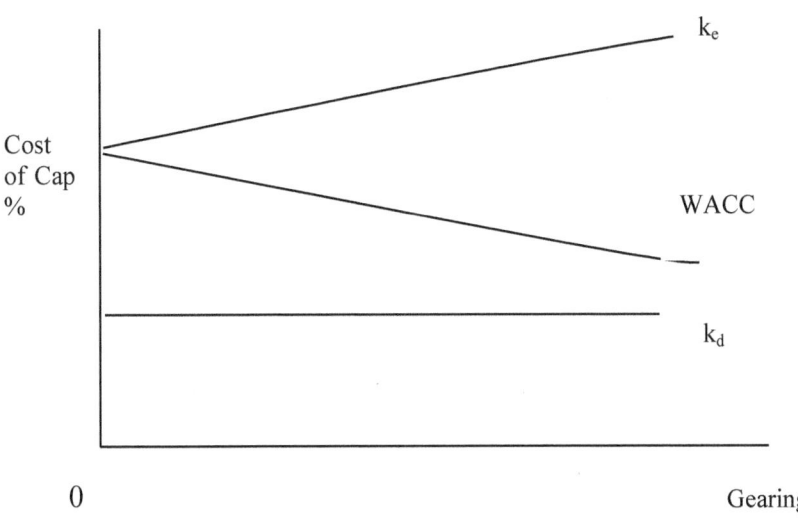

As gearing increases WACC decreases. The higher the level of tax the lower the combined cost of capital becomes (this is not on graph). The higher the level of gearing the more valuable the company becomes.

Further Aspects of the Cost of Capital

There are a few more points to consider when estimating the cost of capital. These do not always figure in calculations but are useful if you are asked to discuss the usefulness of WACC as a tool.

Bankruptcy Costs

The more debt you have the more chance you have of not being able to pay it. To reflect this risk you have to pay high dividends to equity investors.

We can now suggest that:

Market value of firm = Value if all equity financed + value of tax shield (Dt)

Should actually be:

Market value of firm = Value if all equity financed + value of tax shield (Dt) - EPV of bankruptcy costs

Bankruptcy costs: are:

Expected present vale (EPV) of the direct cost of bankruptcy - assets sold below full value, difference between going concern value and straight realisable value of individual assets and the indirect cost of bankruptcy - management time spent dealing with impending crisis, employees leaving, suppliers refusing lines of credit, customers being scared off.

Agency Costs:

It can be assumed that debt holders like the low risk nature of the investment and as such equity holders are by definition slightly less risk averse. In a desperate situation equity holders may be more happy with a risk because they a) will lose out in the case of bankruptcy b) may only have to suffer a loss of dividend c) will be able to claim all of the gain. Debt holders would rather play safe

and still be guaranteed of their return. Managers will generally side with shareholders (although the situation is not quite that simple):
1. Dividends - paying large dividends may keep investors on side
2. Playing for time - managers have a vested interest in keeping the company going, creditors would like it to carry on but if it is going to go it is better sooner than later - as time goes by the company will be worth less and less as they sell off/make cost savings to try to keep going
3. Changing risks - managers may not inform creditors of risky new directions/projects

Loans sometimes have restrictive covenants to avoid (3) - these are part of agency cost.

Restrictions may include:
- No issue of new debt with a superior claim on assets
- Dividend growth may not exceed earnings
- Any merger must maintain levels of asset backing
- Rules concerning investment policy

Tax exhaustion:
The discussion above assumes that interest can be offset against tax. To do this the company must make profits (profit before interest and tax - PBIT) higher than its interest payments. Tax exhaustion occurs when a company has insufficient taxable profits to make use of all the tax relief available to it.

Summary of Modigliani and Miller:

The above discussion can be summarised in the following four charts.

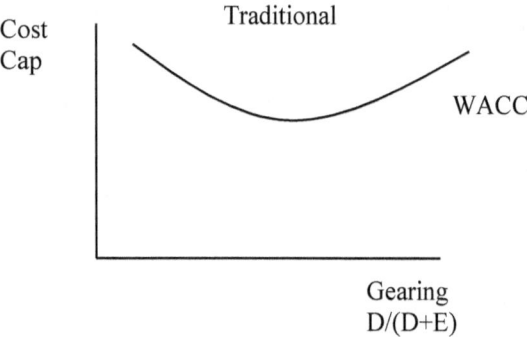

An optimal capital structure exists (a certain balance of debt and equity).

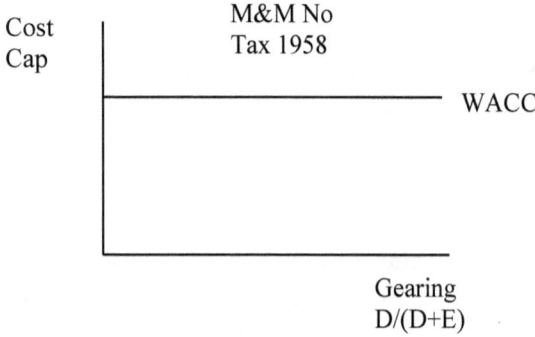

All capital structures are optimal (it does not matter).

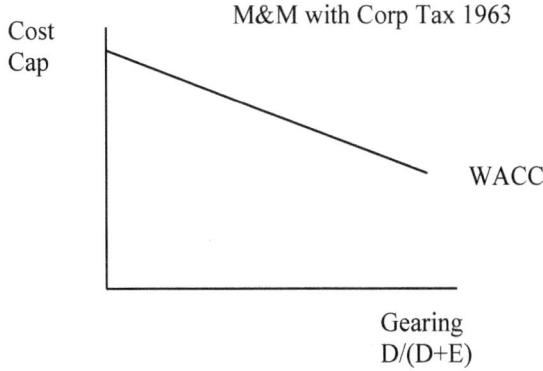

The more gearing the better.

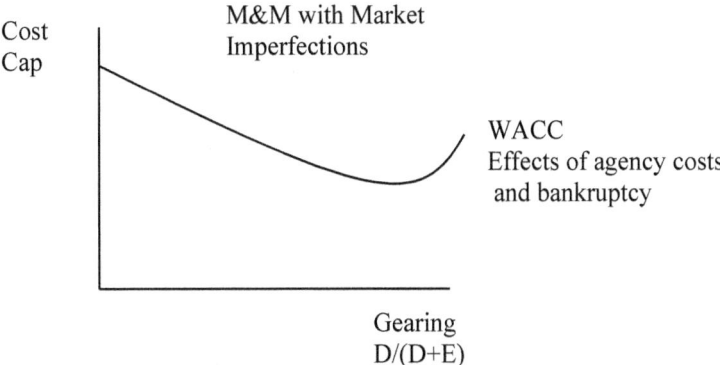

A certain point will be reached where after gearing will become more expensive.

Cost of capital when a company alters gearing

Cost of capital is the return investors require given the present rate of risk. A change in financial risk will necessitate a recalculation of that cost. This can be calculated using the CAPM.

The logic behind using CAPM as cost of capital:

1. Assumed objective is wealth maximisation
2. All investors hold a type of market portfolio
3. The new project is a new investment to add to this portfolio
4. $R_j = R_f + \beta_j(R_m - R_f)$ can be used (β is for the <u>project</u>)
5. We do not look at the project's effect on the company but on the portfolio - only systematic risk - the project's unique risk will disappear by the use of the portfolio

CAPM and Gearing Risk

If gearing is to change we can select a company with similar gearing and risk as the basis of our estimates.

As WACC for a company can be written as:

$$k_{eu} = (k_{eg} \frac{E}{E+D}) + (k_{dg} \frac{D}{E+D})$$

We can re-write it as:

$$\beta_{eu} = (\beta_{eg} \frac{E}{E+D}) + (\beta_{dg} \frac{D}{E+D})$$

β_{eu} is also called the β asset as it has no financial risk (no gearing) We can assume that corporate debt is risk free and so its beta becomes 0 and that term of the equation disappears to give:

$$\beta_{eu} = \beta_{eg} \frac{E}{E+D}$$

Geared company = Business and Financial Risk

Ungeared company = Business Risk

Example allowing for gearing and tax:

Equity beta = 1.5
Ratio is 60% equity and 40% debt
$R_m = 25\%$
$R_f = 10\%$ (which we will use as k_d in this example)
Corporation Tax = 30%
Debt has 0 beta

CAPM:

$k_e = r_f + \beta_{equity}(r_m - r_f)$
$= 10\% + 1.5(25\% - 10\%)$
$= 32.5\%$
Cost of Debt:
$k_d = 10\%(1-t) = 7\%$

WACC:

$$k_{eu} = (k_{eg} \frac{E}{E+D}) + (k_{dg} \frac{D}{E+D})$$
$= (32.5\% \times 0.6) + (7\% \times 0.4)$
$\underline{= 22.3\%}$

Cost of Equity if **ungeared**:
Beta value = $\beta_{eu} = \beta_{eg} \dfrac{E}{E+D(1-t)}$

$$\beta_{eu} = 1.5 \frac{0.6}{0.6 + 0.4(1-0.30)}$$
$= 1.023$
So WACC for an ungeared company is:
$k_e = r_f + \beta_{equity}(r_m - r_f)$
$= 10\% + \mathbf{1.023}(25\% - 10\%)$

= 25.34%

The WACC for the geared is lower than that for the ungeared. Gearing = less cost

In fact the WACC of a geared company is the same as the WACC of an ungeared one modified by one minus the proportion of debt and equity:

$WACC_g = WACC_u(1-(Dt/D+E))$

So:

$WACC_g = 25.34\%$ X $[1-(0.4$ X $0.3)/0.6 + 0.4)]$
= 22.3% (which if you check above is what we calculated)

While this has illustrated the relationship between geared and ungeared cost of capital it can also be used to recalculate the company's WACC with a new level of gearing. By altering the 60/40 split we can see what the new WACC will be after the change in gearing (for example to 80/20):

$WACC_g = 25.34\%$ X $[1-(0.4$ X $0.3)/0.6 + 0.4)]$
Becomes:

$WACC_g = 25.34\%$ X $[1-(0.2$ X $0.3)/0.8 + 0.2)] = 23.82$

Giving:
60/40 Equity/Debt = 22.3
80/20 Equity/Debt = 23.82
All Equity = 25.34

Cost of equity = K₍ₑ₎

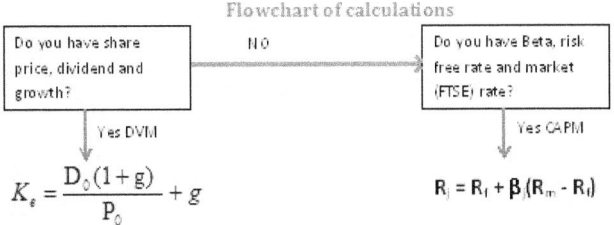

Flowchart of calculations

| Do you have share price, dividend and growth? | NO | → | Do you have Beta, risk free rate and market (FTSE) rate? |

Yes DVM

$$K_e = \frac{D_0(1+g)}{P_0} + g$$

Yes CAPM

$$R_j = R_f + \beta_j(R_m - R_f)$$

Cost of debt = K₍d₎

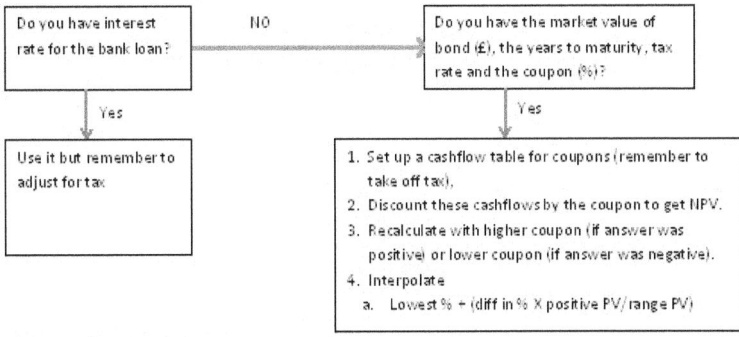

| Do you have interest rate for the bank loan? | NO | → | Do you have the market value of bond (£), the years to maturity, tax rate and the coupon (%)? |

Yes

Use it but remember to adjust for tax

Yes

1. Set up a cashflow table for coupons (remember to take off tax),
2. Discount these cashflows by the coupon to get NPV.
3. Recalculate with higher coupon (if answer was positive) or lower coupon (if answer was negative).
4. Interpolate
   a. Lowest % + (diff in % X positive PV/range PV)

Equity = E (note capital letter E)

1. Work out number of shares in circulation
   a. Book value / par value
2. Read present share price
3. E = number of shares x present share price

Debt = D (note capital letter D)

1. Work out number of bonds in circulation
   a. Book value / £100
2. Read present bond price
3. D = number of bonds x present bond price
4. (Or use book/par x present price)

WACC = weighted average cost of capital

$$WACC = k_e \frac{E}{E+D} + k_d \frac{D}{E+D}$$

Mills (2017) Financial Management made Manageable

Investment Appraisal

Introduction

All decisions in business are investment decisions as they all have implications on resources and cash flows. This section will look directly at those that run over multiple time periods and require some financial outlay (or forfeit). Much of the mathematics in this section has already been covered but it will be reviewed again for those readers who have not needed to look at previous chapters due to their syllabus.

The chapter begins with consideration of which costs are relevant to our decision, this then allows us to calculate the present value of an investment. We will then look at how that can be adjusted to allow for risk and how it can be adjusted to consider the effect of inflation and taxation. We will go on to look at how the internal rate of return is calculated and finally we will look at a couple of alternative methods to judge investments.

Investment considerations

This chapter covers calculations that relate to new investments by a company. As such it is forward looking. This marks a very real difference from financial accounting which tends to report passed events, and management accounting which tends to focus on live costs and revenues. Given this forward looking approach we need to reassess which cost are relevant.

Cost which we have already occurred, whether paid or owed, are termed sunk costs. That is to say that decisions from this point forward will not reduce or remove them. As such they are excluded from our investment decision calculations.

Depreciation is an accounting method not an actual cashflow and so can also be set aside. The purchase price of the asset and its disposal proceeds will be consider in our calculations at the time they occur. To include deprecation as well would be to double count.

Likewise interest cost can be ignored. The WACC we calculated took account of debt interest and to include it again would also be to double count.

Opportunities forgone do need to be considered though. Our choice to do something will shut off other possible activities and any losses from those should be included. For example we may have some old stock that we can use for this project. Its original purchase price is a sunk cost and so can be ignored but what needs to be considered is its replacement cost (if we have another use for it) or its resale (scrap) value if it is of no use (other than this project).

Working capital can be considered but only on an incremental basis. If, for example, £10,000 of working capital per year is required over 5 years then it will only appear as a cost in year 1 and will be repaid in year 5. Values would only appear in the interceding years if there was an increase in working capital and then only the increase not the total amount. Year 5 would then be the sum of these.

Present Value Calculation

The purpose of present value calculation is to convert future cash inflows and outflows into values that are relevant today. Inflation, risk and lost opportunity all erode the value of money over time and to correct this we need to adjust future figures downwards. This has already been discussed in the chapter on the cost of equity but if you have skipped that chapter the discussion goes like this:

Compound interest and discount factors:

Assume an investment of £100 that pays 10% for five years
Year 1 £100 @ 10% = £110
Year 2 £100 @ 10% = £121
Year 3 £121 @ 10% = £133.10
Year 4 £133.10 @ 10% = £146.41
Year 5 £146.41 @ 10% = £161.05

If we use decimals instead of % we can write this as:

£100.00	x	1.10	= £110.00
£110.00	x	1.10	=£121.00
£121.00	x	1.10	=£133.10
£133.10	x	1.10	=£146.41
£146.41	x	1.10	=£161.05

We use 1.1 to represent 100% (1) of the invested money and 10% (0.1) of the return (interest).

Another way of writing the above would be:

£100 x 1.1 x 1.1 x 1.1 x 1.1 x 1.1 = £161.05

And of course the easiest way to write that is:

£161.05 = £100x 1.1^5

This allows us to say that the formal for compound interest is:

$$FV = PV (1+r)^n$$

Where:
FV = future value;
PV = principal value (investment)
r = rate of interest
n = number of years.

Whilst this gives us future value it can also be reversed to give present value:

$$FV = PV (1+r)^n$$

Becomes:

$$PV = \frac{FV}{(1+r)^n}$$

Whilst this allows us to convert a future value to a present one it does not give us a discount factor. A discount factor is a decimal that we can use to convert future values to present values without the use of formula. These are available in tables and are usually provided in examination but if you find yourself needing to produce a spreadsheet or without a table the simplest way is to adjust the formula above:

$$PV = \frac{FV}{(1+r)^n} = FV \frac{1}{(1+r)^n}$$

In the same way that 10/2 is the same as 10 x ½ so the PV can be found by multiplying the future value by $1/(1+r)^n$ instead of dividing it by $(1+r)^n$. As this formula has a limited range of values we would be interested in (n is rarely larger than 20 and r tends to range from 1 to 20) it has been possible to create tables of values. These can be used to multiply future values with to create present values. For example for the above example £161.05 x 0.621 = £100 where 0.621 is the discount factor for five years at 10%:

Cost of capital

Year	2%	3%	4%	5%	6%	7%	8%	9%	10%
1	0.980	0.971	0.962	0.952	0.943	0.935	0.926	0.917	0.909
2	0.961	0.943	0.925	0.907	0.890	0.873	0.857	0.842	0.826
3	0.942	0.915	0.889	0.864	0.840	0.816	0.794	0.772	0.751
4	0.924	0.888	0.855	0.823	0.792	0.763	0.735	0.708	0.683
5	0.906	0.863	0.822	0.784	0.747	0.713	0.681	0.650	0.621
6	0.888	0.837	0.790	0.746	0.705	0.666	0.630	0.596	0.564
7	0.871	0.813	0.760	0.711	0.665	0.623	0.583	0.547	0.513
8	0.853	0.789	0.731	0.677	0.627	0.582	0.540	0.502	0.467
9	0.837	0.766	0.703	0.645	0.592	0.544	0.500	0.460	0.424
10	0.820	0.744	0.676	0.614	0.558	0.508	0.463	0.422	0.386

Present value calculation:

Now suppose a company was to invest £1million now and expected to receive the following cashflows over the five year life of the project:

Year	1	2	3	4	5	Total
Sales	250,000	300,000	400,000	300,000	100,000	
Costs	50,000	80,000	80,000	30,000	10,000	
Net	200,000	220,000	320,000	270,000	90,000	1,100,000

It would seem the sum of the net inflows totals £1,100,000 which is £100,000 more than the initial investment. This seems healthy but misses two vital points.

1. It takes no account of the time value of money
2. It takes no account of investors' expected returns

Inflation alone means that money in the future is worth less than today. Add to that risk and lost opportunity and it does not take much to imagine that this calculation would be more robust if we had some way of adjusting future values downwards to allow for this. Luckily we do and it is rather straightforward. The bottom row (Net) can simply be adjusted using the discount factors calculated above and generally found in a table in the examination. Let's assume the cost of capital for this company is 8%:

Net	200,000	220,000	320,000	270,000	90,000	1,100,000
DF	0.926	0.857	0.794	0.735	0.681	
PV	185,200	188,540	254,080	198,450	61,290	887,560

By multiplying the NET by the discount factor for 8% we now get a present value return of £887,560. The decimal discount factors have made each year's values lower to allow for required return (cost of capital). £887,560 is below the £1million invested and shows that whilst the investors will receive a £100,000 return for the five years they will actually be £112,440 worse off (investment less PV). Their net present value will be negative. They should not invest.

Investors should invest in projects where the NPV is greater than or equal to zero. A zero NPV shows that the required return is met. A NPV higher than zero illustrates a project that will add value to them above and beyond their required return.

Points to note:

1. Only include sales and costs that have yet to be committed. If a cost has already been committed it is considered 'sunk' and has to be paid regardless of whether the project goes ahead. As such it should be ignored.

2. Include opportunity costs. If you have to forego an activity that has a positive revenue to enable you to do this project then include that lost revenue as a cost. If you were about to give up your £10 per hour job to do a £12 per hour job you would think about the loss of £10 to gain £12 – especially if the values were reversed.

3. It is possible that at the end of the project the initial investment may be recouped in part. If it were a machine for example it may have some scrap value. Include this in the final year and discount.

4. All values are year-end values.

5. Woking capital can be included. It is good practice to give this its own line (row). Show the working capital introduced at the start of the project as a cost, each year after only show any increase in working capital (incremental working capital) as the existing working capital is still there. At the end of the project do not forget to reintroduce the working capital is a positive.

With changing WACC

It is possible to have different discount rates in later years. Over time it may be projected that the company's WACC will alter – perhaps due to refinancing planned at a later date altering the ratio for debt and equity or due to expectations about changing cost of debt or equity. It is unusual to find these questions in exams but they do come up.

To alter the discount factor we multiply the new discount factor for one year (the discount factor for year one at 15%) by the discount rate for the previous year (the old discount factor at 10%) - an example will clarify:

Year	DF
0	1
1	0.909 (10%)
2	0.826 (10%)
3	0.870 * 0.826 = 0.71862 (This Year 1 @ 15% * Year 2 @ 10%)

Calculating IRR for these types of projects is possible but will only ever be a crude estimate.

Why does this work? Imagine investing £100 for two years at 10% and then another two years at 15%.

1	100.00	110.00	@10%
2	110.00	121.00	@10%
3	121.00	139.15	@15%
4	139.15	160.02	@15%

Your two years at 15% are built on top of two years at 10%. If you had four years at 15% the value would be higher in years three and four. If you were to try to return from year four to the initial investment by using a 10% discount factor for year four you would get £109.29 as the initial investment – because of course you would need a greater sum to get to the final value. If you discount by 15% for three years you would get £91.50 because four years' worth of 15% can turn a smaller starting value into the final £160.02. By discounting £160.21 by two years of 10% (0.826) and two years of 15% (0.7561) you get the £100 that is correct.

With inflation

The above calculations have all assumed that the values given have been adjusted upwards for inflation. They are in effect the exact amounts that the company would receive at that point.   This is termed 'money' or 'nominal' values. Future values are higher than today and historic values lower.   This is useful as WACC is considered a nominal measure and so must be used with nominal cash flows.

If we are confronted with cashflows that are inflation adjusted (i.e. they are lower as they have had inflation stripped out) then we would need to either re-inflate them or convert our WACC into real terms. We can do this using:

$$(1+r) = \frac{(1+m)}{(1+i)}$$

r = real rate of return

m = money rate of return

i = inflation rate

So if we had a WACC of 15.5% and a rate of inflation of 5% the real WACC would be:

1.155 / 1.05 = 1.1
Or 10%

The real will always be lower than the money. It is of course possible to rearrange this and convert real WACC to money WACC:

1.1 x 1.05 = 1.115
or 15.5%

So in theory, in an examination, you could be asked to discount real cashflows but have been given a nominal WACC or vice versa. To convert a real WACC into a nominal WACC just requires you to remember the formula. However if you are confronted with real cashflows the reverse may not be so easy. It is common to give more than one inflation rate. One for sales and one for costs for example. If this is the case which do you use in the formula? The answer is neither. The more common technique in an exam is to inflate real cashflows. You use the inflation rates to convert the sales and costs into nominal values and then use the WACC given as it is.

To inflate cashflows you use a method similar to the compound interest above. Assuming a 4% inflation rate on the following data and that inflation occurs in year 1 (read the question carefully in the exam):

Year			1	2	3
Units			10,000	15,000	12,000
Sales Price		£5.50			
Inflation		4%	£5.72	£5.95	£6.19
Sales			£57,200	£89,232	£74,241

The sales price is simply increased by 4% each year. This can be done by multiplying by 1.04. This works only when we have a constant value (in this case we know the sales price). If we had sales figures but no sales price it would be slightly more complicated:

We cannot just add 4% each time. If we did we would get this and this is clearly incorrect:

Year		1	2	3
Sales		£55,000	£82,500	£ 66,000
Inflated Sales Price	4%	£57,200.00	£59,488.00	£61,867.52

Instead we should multiply each uninflated sales figure by 1.04 to the power of the year (so year one is 1.04^1; year two is 1.04^2; year three is 1.04^3 etc). Your calculator may have a button for this – if not just multiply the sales by 1.04 as often as required (e.g. for year three £66,000 x 1.04 x 1.04 x 1.04).

Year		1	2	3
Sales		£55,000	£82,500	£66,000
Inflated Sales Price	4%	£57,200.00	£89,232.00	£74,241.02

With taxation

Taxation in investment appraisal presents itself in two forms. First is the recognition that interest payments are tax deductible and that this reduces our cost of capital as discussed above. This is already factored in to the WACC calculation and why we do not include interest payments in the net present value calculation (that and the fact that WACC includes interest). The other is that the company may well be entitled to tax allowances (relief) on its investment. The initial investment, if it was for a machine or some other allowable expense, will mean the company is able to set that expense against taxation. This is normally done in the form of a writing down allowance (WDA) and is most commonly done on a reducing balance basis.

Reducing balance WDA:

Assuming that a machine was bought for £100,000 and that the government allowed a 30% WDA on investments of this type in the year of purchase. Also assume we sold the machine at the end of five years for £30,000:

	Value		WDA		Allowance
1	£100,000	X	30%	=	£30,000
2	£70,000	X	30%	=	£21,000
3	£49,000	X	30%	=	£14,700
4	£34,300	X	30%	=	£10,290
5	£24,010	X	30%	=	£7,203
	£16,807		Total		£83,193

As can be seen at the end of four years the machine was written down to £16,807 (£24,010 less £7,203 or £100,000 less £83,193 whichever you prefer). Each year we would be able to place the allowance value into our calculations and reduce the taxable profit accordingly. In the final year we would have to adjust the allowance by the difference between our sales price and the written down value:

Net	£200,000	£220,000	£320,000	£270,000	£90,000
Allowance	£30,000	£21,000	£14,700	£10,290	£7,203
Adjustment					£13,193
Taxable	£170,000	£199,000	£305,300	£259,710	£95,990

As you can see in the final year the adjustment has been added back in as profit – this is because we sold the machine for more than the government WDA had reduced it to – we had been over compensated by allowances (the machine was written down to £16,807 but we sold it for £30,000 – a difference of £13,193). If we had sold the machine for less than £16,807 that amount would have been used to further reduce our taxable profit (it would be added to the allowance rather than taken away).

If we assume a tax rate of 20% and that tax is payable one year in arears we see our net profit after tax (PAT) as:

A	Net	200,000	220,000	320,000	270,000	90,000	
	WDA	£30,000	£21,000	£14,700	£10,290	£7,203	
	Adj'					£13,193	
	Net	£170,000	£199,000	£305,300	£259,710	£95,990	
B	Tax		£34,000	£39,800	£61,060	£51,942	£19,198
C	PAT	£200,000	£186,000	£280,200	£208,940	£38,058	-£19,198

It is important to remember that the Net PAT is the Net less the tax paid (nothing to do with the taxable profit – students often make this mistake). C = A-B. Also note that the net received in the first year has no tax as none has been paid yet (remember this is actual cashflow not income statement). In year two year one's tax is paid and in year three years two's and so on. Finally in year six tax is paid for year five though there is no income.

This Net PATis then discounted using discount factors as above to give NPV.

Internal Rate of Return (IRR)

The IRR is the cost of capital at which the project produces an NPV of £0. It is the maximum the project can bear before there would be losses in expected value for investors. As such the maths is very similar to that used for bonds and debentures above:

Our investment appraisal will have given us an NPV. From the example earlier it was:

Net	£200,000	£220,000	£320,000	£270,000	£90,000	
DF	0.926	0.857	0.794	0.735	0.681	
PV	£185,200	£188,540	£254,080	£198,450	£61,290	£887,560

Invest	£1,000,000
PV	£887,560
NPV	(£112,440)

So a WACC of 10% left us with an NPV of (£112,440). Clearly the IRR must be lower than this as the project cannot make a surplus paying this much in capital charges. We can try again using 2% (in the exam just make a sensible guess – if you end up with another negative value you just have to redo with a lower WACC).

Net	£200,000	£220,000	£320,000	£270,000	£90,000	
DF	0.9804	0.9612	0.9423	0.9238	0.9057	
PV	£196,080	£211,464	£301,536	£249,426	£81,513	£1,040,019

Invest	£1,000,000
PV	£1,040,019
NPV	£40,019

We now have four values. At 10% we have an NPV of (£112,440) and at 2% an NPV of £40,019. The actual IRR is somewhere between these two values. A mathematical technique called interpolation can be used to determine the exact value.

If we were to visualise what we are trying to do it would look like this:

2%	?%	10%
£40,019	£0	(£112,440)

We are aiming to determine the % that will give us £0 and show that then cashflow in exactly balances the original cashflow out.

The value will be at least 2%, in addition it will be somewhere between 2% and 10%. So it will be 2% plus some fraction of the difference between 2% and 10% (i.e. some fraction of 8%).

This can be written as:

$$IRR = 2\% + \left[8\% \times \frac{£40,019}{£40,019 + £112,440} \right] = 4.1\%$$

Notice that the minus sign has been dropped from the £112,440 this is because the range between £40,019 and (£112,440) is what is required.

$$IRR = \text{lowest \%} \left[\text{difference in \%} \times \frac{\text{Positive NPV}}{\text{Range of NPV}} \right]$$

It is worth noting that this is IRR by linear interpolation and as such is an estimate. Luckily it is one close enough for practical purposes:

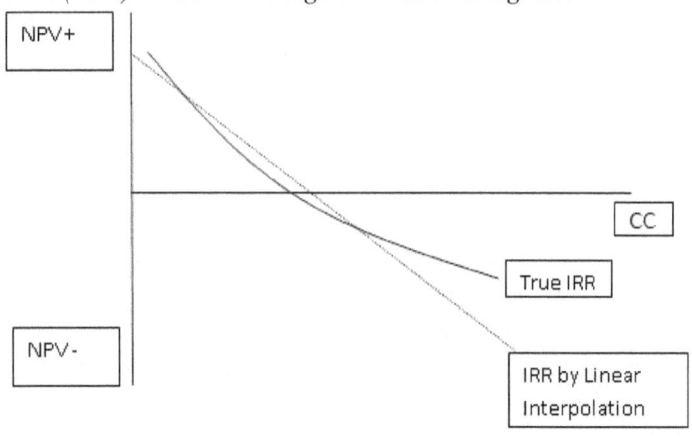

Accounting Rate of Return (ARR)

ARR simply compares annual profit increase with the initial investment. The company will have a policy for the acceptable ARR.

$$ARR = \frac{\text{Average profit (after depreciation + tax)}}{\text{Average capital invested}}$$

Where:
Average Profit = sum of profits during the projects life ÷ years
Average Capital Invested = Investment ÷ 2
(This may be opening investment +closing investment ÷2 if relevant or if investment occurs each year it is total investment divided by number of years)

In many ways this is similar to Return on Investment. We are comparing what we put in and what we got out.

However ARR is:

- Not directly related to wealth maximisation - but accounting profit maximisation

- Ignores timing of flows (front end loading ignored)

- Ignores time value of money.

- Can cause problems due to the use of accounting information (attributed costs, depreciation etc. which are not actual cashflows but are determined by internal company policy)

Payback Period

This is the easiest method and asks the question: "When will the investment be repaid by cashflows?"

If we invest £1,000 and receive £100 per year the payback period (PBP) is 10 years.

If the receipts were £150 the PBP would be:
£15 * 6 years = £900
and £150 ÷ £100 (the difference betwenn the £900 so far and the £1,000 needed)= 0.66 years or 8 months.   In other words 6 years 8 months.

The company will have a policy concerning what it considers to be a reasonable PBP.

However PBP is flawed, it makes no account of inflation or interest rates. In addition it makes the assumption that speedy repayments represents reduced risk - which is only true up to a point. In addition cashflows after the investment have occurred are ignored - but these can be very important:

Investment Cashflows
P1 (£1,000)   £250 £250 £250 £250 £250 end
P2 (£1,000)   £100 £150 £250 £300 £300 £400 £350 end

PBP would indicate that P1 was the better investment but which would you prefer?

Risk adjusted

We should always be nervous that our estimates may be over generous. If sales are lower than expected and cost higher we have a **down side risk**.

It would be useful if we could target those key variables that, if changed, cause us losses. It easy to see that some values may be more **sensitive** than others.

The weakness of this approach is that we can only look at one variable at a time - which is not very realistic. Also it does not actual asses risk but rather suggests which may be the key variable. However it is a practical and usable method for beginning a conversation about risk.

Sensitivity Example:

Cost of Capital 12%	= CC
Investment £7m	= I
Price per unit £10	= S
Cost per unit £6	= VC
Volume 800,000	= N
Project	= 4 years

$NPV = ((S-VC) * N * CC_{12,4}) - I$
($CC_{12,4}$ means cost of capital at 12% for 4 years)
Which just says NPV equals ((sales price less sales cost) times number sold times discount factor) less investment

As with discount factors there are annuity tables which allow us to discount future values based on a cost of capital. These tables can only be used when the cashflow is the same each year and replace the need to do calculations for each year with a single calculation. They can be used here to represent the impact of cost of capital.

	7%	8%	9%	10%	11%	12%
1	0.9346	0.9259	0.9174	0.9091	0.9009	0.8929
2	1.8080	1.7833	1.7591	1.7355	1.7125	1.6901
3	2.6243	2.5771	2.5313	2.4869	2.4437	2.4018
4	3.3872	3.3121	3.2397	3.1699	3.1024	3.0373
5	4.1002	3.9927	3.8897	3.7908	3.6959	3.6048

If we look up in this table 12% for 4 years we see a discount value of 3.0373.

This gives us:

NPV = ((10-6.00) * 800,000 * 3.0373) - 7,000,000 = £2,719,517

Now, if we were to try to get to an NPV of 0 this would give us an idea of sensitivity. To do this for a variable simple set NPV to zero and rearrange:

Initial Investment:
$0 = ((10\text{-}6.00) * 800,000 * 3.0373) - I$
$0+I = ((10\text{-}6.00) * 800,000 * 3.0373)$
$I_{max} = £9,719,517$

This is an increase of £2,719,518 or 38.85% - this is how much the investment could increase in price by for us to still make money

Sales Price:
$0 = ((S\text{-}6.00) * 800,000 * 3.0373) - 7,000,000$
$7,000,000 = (S\text{-}6.00) * 800,000 * 3.0373$
$7,000,000 / (800,000 * 3.0373) = S - 6$
$6 + (7,000,000 / (800,000 * 3.0373)) = S$
$S_{min} = £8.88$

A decrease of £1.12 or 11.2%

Variable Cost:
As this is directly related to profit (via price) it has the same result 11.2%

Sales Volume:
$0 = ((10\text{-}6.00) * N * 3.0373) - 7,000,000$
$7,000,000 = ((10\text{-}6.00) * N * 3.0373)$

7,000,000 / ((10-6.00) = N * 3.0373)
7,000,000 / 4 = N x 3.0373
1,750,000 = N x 3.0373
1,750,000 / 3.0373 = N
N_{min} = 576,160
A decrease of 223,840 or 28%

Discount Rate:
0 = ((10-6.00) * 800,000 * CC) - 7,000,000
7,000,000 = ((10-6.00) * 800,000 * CC)
7,0000,000 / 4 = 800,000 x CC
1,750,000 / 800,000 = 2.19
CC_{max} = 2.19

2.19 translates to 29% on an annuity table. An absolute increase of 17% which is a 142% increase in the actual rate.

	25%	26%	27%	28%	29%	30%
1	0.8000	0.7937	0.7874	0.7813	0.7752	0.7692
2	1.4400	1.4235	1.4074	1.3916	1.3761	1.3609
3	1.9520	1.9234	1.8956	1.8684	1.8420	1.8161
4	2.3616	2.3202	2.2800	2.2410	2.2031	2.1662

From the above you can see that the Price/Cost is most sensitive to change. Small percentage changes quickly give us an NPV of 0.

Investment – 38.85% increase
Sales – 11.2% fall
Costs – 11.2% increase
Volume – 28% fall
Cost of capital – 142% increase

You can see that the project is most sensitive to a change in price or costs, next most sensitive to a change in volume, then initial investment and finally to the cost of capital.

If you enjoy spreadsheets it is possible to set up an NPV on a spreadsheet such that all of the variables above are in independent cells. You can then confirm the results above by setting the values to those calculated and demonstrating that the NPV is indeed near zero each time.

Risk-adjustment:

We have already talked about the fact that cost of capital includes some allowance of time value of money and some allowance for risk. This seems to suggest that more risky projects should have a higher cost of capital. We could decide on project "riskiness" and then select an appropriate cost of capital. Alternatively we could use the WACC. You could also suggest that higher rates are need in early years to reflect the newness of the venture.

Probability and NPV:

We can alter are cashflows to represent best case, most likely case and worst case. We can then assign a probability to each (obviously most likely is the highest) Say 0.2, 0.7 and 0.1 (best case, likely case, worst case)

NOTE: be careful, you may see probabilities mention and they may only refer to a single element. It may be possible to calculate the expected outcome for this element rather than do several NPVs. If we then determine three NPVs reflecting the three situations we only have to times each NPV by its probability to get to the expected NPV (eNPV).

	P	NPV	eNPV
Best	0.2	£30,000	£6,000
Likely	0.7	£20,000	£14,000
Worst	0.1	£10,000	£1,000
eNPV			£21,000

Of course this is still just an estimate.

Mills (2017) Financial Management made Manageable

Managing Risk

Introduction

There are various methods that businesses use to manage risk and this depends largely on the type of risk. Risk can range from litigation (often managed by effective risk assessments and safety policies) to physical risks of theft and fire. From a financial perspective risk is normally separated into business risk and financial risk. Business risk is the unique risk associated with that industry (for example the difference between running an oil well and a bakery) while financial risk focuses on the risk introduced by gearing. The greater the proportion of debt the greater the risk of corporate failure. Added to these are the risk associated with dealing in foreign currencies and this will be the focus of this chapter.

Any business that trades internationally will be exposed to exchange rate risk in some way. This may be through exporting or importing or through actually having operations that are located in other currency areas. We separate these exchange rate risks into three types:

Transaction Exposure

- Gains or losses as the result of having entered into a contract involving payment or receipt of money at a future date in different currencies. Protection is often through hedging.

Translation Exposure

- The need for a multinational company to state all of its operators in its home currency.

Economic Exposure

- The present value of an international company's future cash flows is exposed to currency movements. Foreign devaluation will lead to a reduction in the value of repatriated profits, but also an export potential for the subsidiary.

Relative Importance of Different Exposures

Transaction exposure and economic exposure are the same ultimately (time scale different) and they both affect cash flow. Translation exposure really just affects balance sheet values.

Exchange Rates

In order to determine ways to reduce this risk it is first helpful to gain a deeper understanding of currency. When a foreign currency depreciates this is favourable for an exporter and adverse for an importer. Likewise when a foreign currency appreciates this is favourable for an importer and adverse for an exporter. The change in currency will have increased or decreased the price of the product for an exporter and increased or decreased the cost of a product for an importer – but both cannot gain or lose at the same time. It si what is called a zero sum game.

Spot and Forward Exchange Rates

The spot rate is the current rate of exchange; the forward rate is the rate at which dealers will exchange currencies at some future specified date. We will go on to see that this is one method of managing currency risk.

Spot rate:

$1.6600	-	$1.6700
Broker Sells		Broker Buys
$s to us		$s from us
Turn £ to $		Turn $ to £

The sell price is lower than the buy because we are based in pounds, not dollars. They will sell you less dollars for a pound than they will give you. This is how they make their profit.

This could also be expressed in £s to $s:

£0.602 - £0.5988
Sells   Buys

They will sell you one dollar for £0.602 and buy it back for £0.5988

To change $30,000 into pounds gives you £17,964 ($30,000/$1.67)

To get $30,000, you need £18,072.29 ($30,000/$1.6600)

Forward rate:

If we know we need money in the future, we can use a forward rate. A forward rate is a future exchange rate that the bank is willing to offer you now. You enter into a contract which fixes the price. This is termed a forward rate agreement (FRA).

1. Outright quote:

Spot rate $1.6600 - $1.6700
1 month $1.6550 - $1.6675

The forward rate has a wider spread than spot to reflect dealer risk.

2. Premium quote:

If sterling is weakening in the future, dollars will be at a premium - if it was appreciating, dollars would be at a discount.

Thus the above could be written:

$/£ 1 month forward   0060 cents - 0025 cents premium

Spot rate - premium = outright quote

Premiums are sometimes called cpm and discounts dis.

To get to a forward rate from a spot rate you must add discounts or deduct premiums.

Spot rate $1.6600 - $1.6700
$/£ 1 month forward   0060 cents - 0025 cents dis

Would give $30,000 / (1.67 + 0.0025) = £17,937

One way of managing risk therefore is to enter into a forward rate agreement. This guarantees the exchange rate at a fixed point in the future. Although it is likely that you will have a less favourable rate than sport at that time uncertainty has been removed and you can predict cashflows with more confidence. Risk has reduced.

The Determination of Exchange Rates

Currencies change because there are changes in trade either increasing demand for or reducing demand for the currency (caused perhaps by a change in balance of payments - BoP) and/or because capital is moved between different countries, partly due to changes in interest rates and inflation.

Purchasing Power Parity

The law of one price states that in the absence of barriers and transaction costs, the same good will cost the same in all markets (there will be parity). The arbitrage process ensures this.

$$S_{t+1}^{e} = S_0 \; x \; \frac{(1+\dot{p}^*)}{(1+\dot{p})} \qquad \dot{p}^* = \text{inflation in US}$$

$$\dot{p} = \text{inflation in UK}$$

The future expected spot price is the existing spot price multiplied by one plus foreign inflation divided by one plus national inflation. This expected spot forms the forward rate offered by banks (adjusted to allow for a return).

Of course, this ignores capital movements, includes only those goods that are traded internationally and ignores governments' attempts to manage exchange rates. However, it is a useful long-term economic model.

Interest Rate Models

The above express currency changes in relation to inflation but interest rates also have an impact. It can be suggested that interest rates contain two elements - return and a premium to cover inflation.

If the real rate of return is the same in all countries, then differences in nominal rates will reflect differences in inflation - this is called the International Fisher Effect. Where countries have not properly taken account of inflation, then there will be capital flows. Countries with high real rates of interest will see appreciating currencies and low real rates depreciating. This leads on to the interest rate parity model.

The interest rate parity model suggests that nominal exchange rate differences can predict exchange rate movements. If forward exchange rates for sterling against the dollar were no higher than spot, but US nominal interest rates were higher, the following would occur:

1. UK investors would shift funds to the US, receive higher interest on those funds and then exchange back to sterling back with no loss.
2. The flow of capital would raise UK interest rates and force up spot.
3. The difference has therefore predicted the change in spot.

$$S^e_{t+1} = S_0 \times \frac{(1+r^*)}{(1+r)}$$

$r^* = $ interest rate in US
$r = $ interest rate in UK

As can be seen this is much the same as the PPP model. In fact both models suggest similar responses to changes. In the case of interest increases lead to devaluation as it is assumed they signal expected increases in inflation.

Currency Invoicing Decisions

You may decide to manage currency risk by invoicing your customer in your own currency. However this may well impact on sales/marketing.

Mills (2017) Financial Management made Manageable

In order we normally prefer: Own currency, currency stable with ours, market leader's currency, other currency with good forward rate.

Whereas the buyer prefers: Own currency, currency stable with own, other currency they have/earn, currency their other suppliers use.

Lead Payment Option

There is nothing to stop you paying a bill in advance (lead payment) – paying after it is due may be more difficult but still possible (lag payment). This gives you more control over when the bill is paid and therefore you can opt for a more favourable exchange rate.

Money Market Hedge

If we are due to receive \$10,000 in 5 years' time and if American interest rates are 10% then in theory we could borrow \$6,209.2 now at a cost of ($10,000)/ $(1 + 0.1)^5$.

Our payment in 5 years' time will pay off the loan but we get \$6,209.2 today at today's exchange rate. This reduces risk, allows us to have certainty around our cashflows and allows us to reinvest the money.

Futures Contracts:

Futures contracts are for a fixed amount and a fixed maturity date. It is tradable and so the value of the 'right to buy or sell' in itself goes up and down. You enter into a futures contract not to guarantee a rate but to compensate you if the rate goes against you. If the rate is favourable you pay out most of your gain. This differs from a FRA. You are not entering into an arrangement to buy or sell currency. You are instead 'betting' on the changes in currency such that if the currency moves against you 'bet' will pay out an amount that covers your loss. Likewise if the currency moves in your favour you have funds to pay off your 'betting' loss. This is referred to as hedging as you are protected in both directions.

For example, if there were such a thing as a derivative market for houses it may look something like this:

Today's house price £200,000

FRA – you agree to buy that house for £210,000 in 12 months.

Option – you pay £2,000 premium for the right to buy a house of that type for £210,000 in 12 months. If houses prices are lower you let it lapse and although you have paid out £2,000 'unnecessarily' you are relived that the market is now at a price lower than expected. If houses prices are higher than £210,000 you are paid the difference and have that cash to put toward the higher price.

Futures contract – you take a position that they will be £210,000 against someone who believes they will lower. If they are higher you receive the difference – if they are lower you pay the difference (but of course also now pay less than £210,000 for the house so have some spare capital).

Analysis of futures contracts remains a central part of most advanced courses of study in financial management though you may not find them on an undergraduate business degree. Questions of this type will often ask the cost of the futures contract when it is 'closed out' – that is when it is ended before its date.

When calculating the value of a futures contract at point t, its margin, the gain or its efficiency we usually use some form of the following (simplified) process:

1. **Select month closest to required date**

2. **Calculate number of contracts required:**

Investment amount
Contract size

3. **Calculate basis:**

Spot price – futures price = basis

4. **Calculate basis at date contract is closed out:**

Basis * Months left
Total futures' months

5. **Determine expected price of future at point *t***

Spot – Basis at *t* = Futures Price
Margin = difference between this and original price

6. **Determine futures gain (loss)**

Margin * contracts * contract size
7. **Calculate efficiency of hedge**

Profit on futures contract
Loss on spot

Whilst students are usually able to follow this process with positive results it is also apparent that an understanding of what is happening and why is sometimes missing. The following question is solved using the above approach and represented graphically.

Question:

Assume today is June 30th. An amount of money is owed by an American company trading in dollars to a Japanese company trading in Yen. The money (¥100m) is due on the 1st of September.

Current spot price is $/¥128.10 ($0.007806).
Future Contracts exist per ¥12,500,000 settled on 30th.
Sept. 0.007884 premium (¥126.84)
Dec. 0.008334 premium (¥199.99)
Spot price on September 1st is ¥120

---

1. Select month closest to required date
September

2. Calculate number of contracts required:

$$\frac{¥100m}{¥12.5m} = 8$$

3. Calculate basis:

¥128.10 – ¥126.84 = ¥1.26

4. Calculate basis at date contract is closed out:

$$¥1.26 * \frac{1}{3} = ¥0.42$$

5. Determine expected price of future at point *t*

¥120 – ¥0.42 = ¥119.58 ($0.008363)

Margin is $0.008363 - $0.007884 = $0.0004786

6. Determine futures gain (loss)

$0.0004786 * 8 * 12,500,000 = $47,860

7. Calculate efficiency of hedge

$$\frac{\$47,860}{(¥200m\,/¥120) – (¥200m/¥128.10)} = 45.4\%$$

The same problem can be represented with a simple diagram that captures the decay in value over time. This is very similar to the way we depreciate assets.

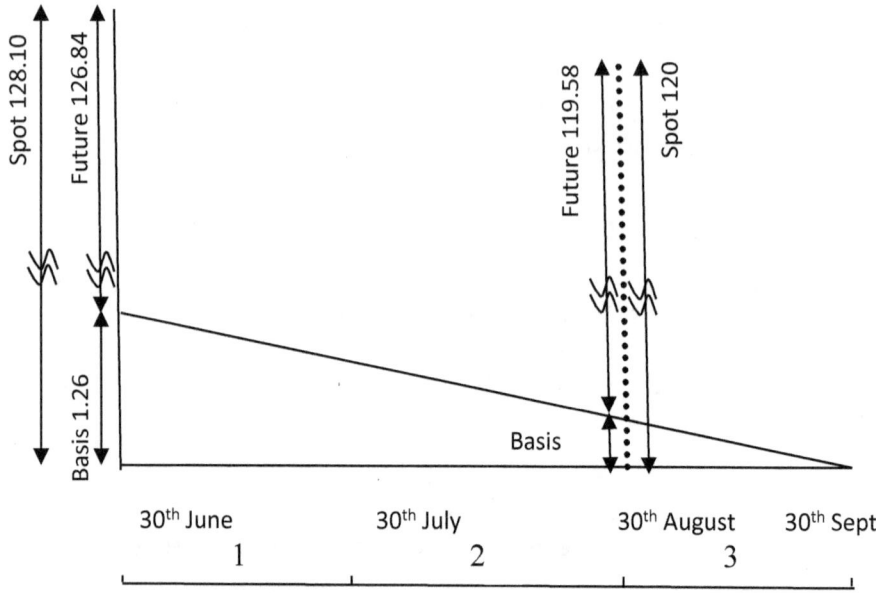

In addition to this overall representation it is possible to use charts to solve part of the calculation. If the determination of basis value at point t (30th August) is considered then the construction of a chart on graph paper will produce a value that can be read from a suitable scale. Clearly though this method will be less accurate than a numerical approach due to the difficulty of clearly drawing and reading scales. However it should provide a good approximation as a check to your maths.

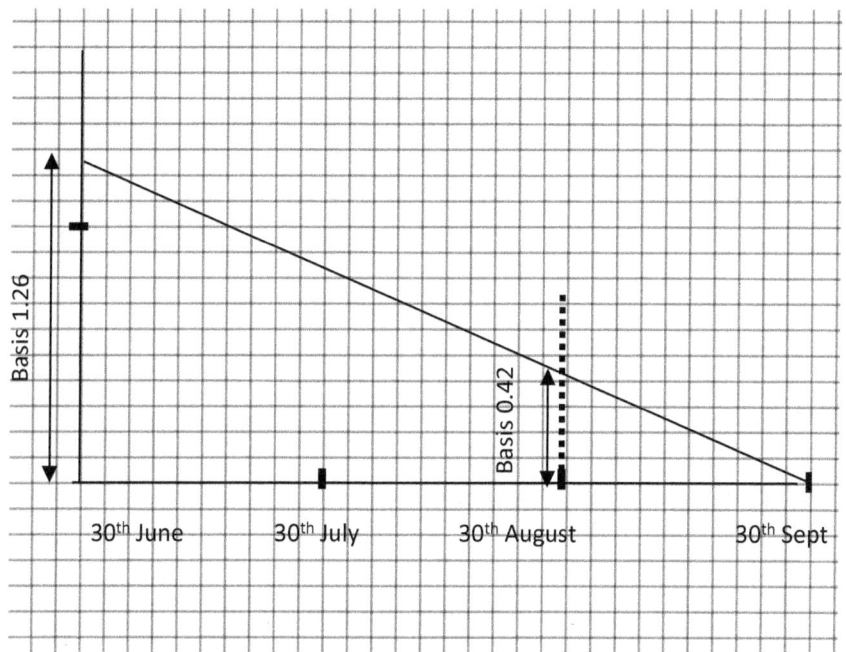

Options Contract

Rather than buy forward by x months the option contract offers the option to buy at a certain price at a certain time. You have to pay a cost for this option, and these options can themselves be traded. But if when the time comes the currency markets are in your favour you can let the option expire. Alternatively you can exercise the option.   The right to buy is a 'call' option and the right to sell a 'put'.   Calculation with these options only involves consideration of the premium.

$160,000 is payable to us on 1st December.

Options available:

| 1 December | $1.60 call | premium £600 per contract |
| 1 December | $1.60 put | premium £500 per contract |

Contract size is £25,000

Hedge

We need to 'call in' some sterling at a good dollar price:

$$\frac{\$160,000}{\$1.60} = £100,000$$

$$\frac{£100,000}{£25,000} = 4 \text{ contracts}$$

We now have the right to buy £100,000 for $160,000 should this be advantageous (on 1st December) (but we paid out 4 x £600)

Depending on currency spot at 1st December we can:

| $1.20/£ | abandon | $160,000/1.20 – (£2,400) = £130,933 |
| $1.60 | either | $160,000/1.60 – (£2,400) = £97,600 |

$2.00/£   exercise $160,000/1.60 – (£2,400) = £97,600

No option

$2.00/£   convert $160,000/2 = £80,000

We have limited what we will receive to a minimum of £97,600. Without this protection it would have fallen to £80,000.

PUT OPTION

We gain with PUT options when values are below (to the left of) our option exchange value.

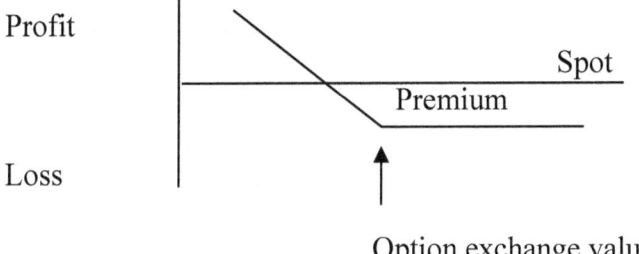

CALL

We gain with CALL options when values are above (to the right of) our option.

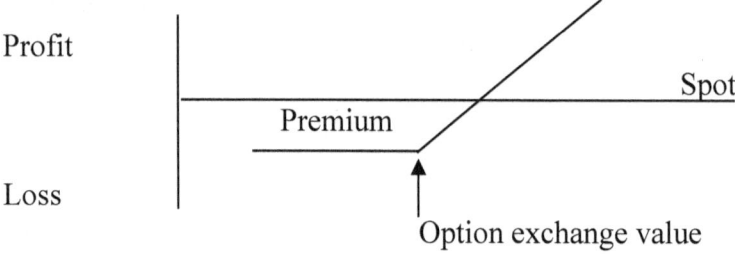

Options contracts premiums and prices are determined using models such as Black–Scholes. This model is beyond the scope of this text. While a company's treasury function may make use of FRAs, futures contracts or options contracts it is unlikely that it will be involved in writing them. The company will be using these instruments to manage risk not as a source of income. It is of course possible to enter into these agreements without needing the underlying asset (the currency) – in effect what you are doing is betting on the movement of the market. Again this type of speculation is a specialist area outside of the scope of a text that examines routine business practice.

Index